Famous Children

BACH

Ann Rachlin
ILLUSTRATED BY Susan Hellard

BARRON'S

Johann Sebastian Bach's father and mother died in 1694, when he was almost ten. He went to live in his big brother's house. His brother Christophe took good care of him. He sent him to school and, each day when Johann Sebastian came home, he would give him a lesson on the clavier, a keyboard instrument something like a piano. Johann loved music more than anything.

Christophe was a composer and played the organ at Ohrduff where they lived. He was very strict and would only allow Johann Sebastian to practice for one hour every day. The little boy hated to hear the words,

"That's enough for today, Johann. Now go and do your arithmetic and the rest of your homework!"

"Boring! Boring!" Johann Sebastian grumbled to himself as he went off.

When he left the music room each day, Johann Sebastian would look up at Christophe's music in the cabinet, which was always locked. The tall cabinet had crossed wooden bars covering the shelves. Through the bars Johann could see that very special book. Oh! How he longed to hold it in his hands!

Johann Sebastian knew that the book was full of exciting music. The pieces Christophe gave him to play were easy and he knew them by heart. He begged Christophe for new music. But the reply was always the same.

It wasn't fair. He would be especially careful with that book. So why was Christophe so worried?

"Oh, please, Christophe, don't say no! I won't hurt it! I promise!"

Little Johann's face would crinkle in disappointment as his big brother sternly shook his head.

"Not yet! You're not old enough! And I don't want your grubby fingermarks all over my best music book!"

It was late. Johann Sebastian lay in his bed but he could not sleep. The book filled his thoughts. He heard Christophe go to bed. Soon the house was dark and quiet. He sat up in bed.

"Maybe I can just look at that book!" he thought. He tiptoed to the bedroom door.

It was very cold and he shivered. Slowly, he eased the door open and crept out on the landing.

He could hear his brother's heavy breathing. Christophe was fast asleep.

He crossed the landing to the top of the stairs.

Now to get down them quietly!

Holding onto the bannister, he went down one step – then another. He reached the bottom of the stairs, his heart beating furiously.

Silently he went toward the music room. The door was closed and the handle slipped in his moist hand. He wiped his hand on his nightshirt and opened the door.

The curtains were open and the full moon was shining in on the cabinet – and that precious book.

Johann Sebastian quietly pulled the door closed behind him and went to the bookcase. There – he could see the book above his head. He stretched up, but he was far too small!

He looked around the room. A chair! That's what he needed! Very carefully, he carried a chair across the room and quietly put it down in front of the music cabinet. Then, without making a sound, he climbed onto the chair, and lifted his arm to reach the top shelf. Even on tiptoes, it was no good. He was still too small.

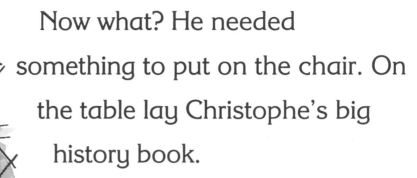

Now what? He needed something to put on the chair. On the table lay Christophe's big history book.

"Just what I need," thought Johann Sebastian and scrambled down to get it. He lifted the book onto the chair. Once again he climbed onto the edge, then onto the book. He could just reach Christophe's precious music book. Squeezing his hands in between the bars, he managed to slip it out.

There – at last he had it in his hands. Johann Sebastian climbed down and put the history book and the chair back where they belonged. With the music book clutched tightly in his hands, he made his way upstairs to the safety of his room.

In the bright moonlight he could read the music easily. It was beautiful. He had to have it. There was only one thing to do. He got out his pen, ink and manuscript paper and, by the light of the moon, he set to work copying down every single note.

Just before sunrise, he hid his precious sheets of manuscript paper under his mattress. Retracing his steps downstairs, he carefully put Christophe's book back on the shelf.

Christophe would never know.

Wearily he climbed the stairs again, got into bed and fell fast asleep.

It seemed only five minutes later when Christophe hammered on the door calling,

"Johann, why aren't you up? You'll be late for school! Hurry up!"

Johann Sebastian Bach fell asleep at his desk that day. The teacher was not at all pleased. Johann was so tired that he even made mistakes at the clavier and Christophe was angry with him too. But Johann Sebastian put up with the scolding. He had his secret and nothing would stop him.

The next night the moon shone again and Johann Sebastian crept downstairs to the music room. Every night for six long months he worked on, climbing the stairs with the precious book, copying all the thousands of notes, until he was finished.

As he placed the book back in the cabinet for the last time, he jumped down from the chair and smiled happily.

"Now it is mine! I can't wait to play every piece for myself when Christophe is out!" He hurried back upstairs and, placing his copy under the mattress, he slept soundly till morning.

It was a lovely spring morning and, after breakfast, Christophe announced,

"I am going to the church to practice for the service next Sunday. I'll be back in an hour or so."

Johann Sebastian could hardly wait for him to go. He heard the front door close and, after waiting for a few minutes, he ran upstairs, grabbed his music sheets and flew downstairs into the music room.

Soon he was at the clavier, playing from his own copy of Christophe's special book. He was so engrossed in the music that he did not hear the front door open as Christophe returned for his coat.

He nearly jumped out of his skin when a furious voice behind him thundered,

"So you disobeyed me! You have my book! Give it to me at once!"

"No, Christophe, it's not your book! Oh, please Christophe, I didn't hurt it! Honestly, I didn't!"

Christophe marched over to the clavier and saw the careful copy of his book.

"I see. You copied it. Very well, now you will see what happens to disobedient boys. Give it to me!"

"No, Christophe, don't take it from me! It's mine!" wailed poor Johann Sebastian.

His elder brother grabbed the precious manuscript and strode out of the room, saying,

"I will not tolerate disobedience. You will never see these pages again." The front door slammed.

Johann Sebastian sat at the clavier, tears rolling down his cheeks. All that work! Wasted! He placed his hands on the keys and began to play. It was the first piece he had copied. Slowly a smile spread across his face. He sat up straight and his fingers flew across the keyboard. Now he was laughing out loud. He remembered every single note he had written down. All the music was locked safely in his memory. Christophe could never take it away from him. It was his forever.